A GROWNUP'S GARDEN OF VIRTUES:

*Inspirational Poems
by Dr. Bill*

William Carroll, Ph. D.

TABLE OF CONTENTS

INTRODUCTION

By Sheri Bailey

Author of *Summers in Suffolk, A Great and Dismal Swamp,* and other stage and screen plays; founder of Hampton Roads Juneteenth Festival, Inc., and of The Juneteenth Players.

In this world full of gadgets, gizmos and gigabytes, William Carroll's gentle encouragement to stop and smell the roses is a lighthouse beacon on a foggy night. Progress has given us the ability to microwave a cake in six minutes. We no longer have time to preheat the oven, flour the pans, mix the ingredients, pour the batter and lick the spoon as we enjoy the divine aroma of a delicious melt-in-your-mouth treat as a reward for a job well done. Progress has given us the ability to watch 24/7, without interruption, multiple television programs and keep up with global news via an information crawl at the bottom of the screen. Progress has given us everything we want with scant attention paid to what we need. And what we need is to connect to an appreciation for a kinder, simpler life.

Bill Carroll's appreciation for writing and vegetable gardening is exactly the salve needed to heal our wounded souls. No two better pursuits could be found that serve the twofold purpose of nurturing and sustaining mind, body and spirit. The healing joy of digging in rich, dark soil with one's bare hands is often left behind with childhood, but for those of us who no longer have time for such nonsense – we who probably need it most – it is an experience that cannot be described, but only understood through doing. As for writing, the transformative experience of finding words to express emotion and experience allows mere human beings to create something pure and precious.

Both vegetable gardening and creative writing can result in tangible products that give back intangible, immeasurable gifts. No one can buy the satisfaction of sharing home-grown vegetables with family and friends or knowing that hungry strangers will be fed. Only those who write can appreciate a poem or journal entry that captures exactly an emotion or idea preserved for posterity like a photograph or memory to be returned to when needed. Bills' poems, like the fruits and vegetables he so generously shares with others (in his neighborhood, his church, or the local food bank) provide delight and nourishment for those who receive them.

Fortunately, William Carroll's willingness to share his mid-life epiphanies is available to those of us looking to get off life's treadmill and experience a kinder, simpler existence. Thank you, Dr. Bill.

- Sheri Bailey
Portsmouth, VA

AUTHOR'S PREFACE AND FOREWORD

I chose to call this collection *A Grownup's Garden of Virtues: Inspirational Poems by Dr. Bill* for several interrelated reasons. It deals with two of my favorite retirement activities: writing and vegetable gardening. Furthermore, I consider all the pieces in this volume inspirational in some way. They are certainly inspirational to me if to no one else. I think most of them will prove to be inspiring to most readers, even if they do not inspire the response I expected or desired.

In my seventies, I do a lot of thinking about the meaning and value of life. I try to put some of these thoughts into poems that will be accessible to a variety of readers with differing religious beliefs (or lack thereof). I do not expect or demand that readers agree with my ideas, just that they comprehend and consider them.

I do not set out to promote a particular set of religious beliefs, but rather make an attempt to put forth ideas that might appeal to people of good conscience regardless of their religious preferences. It does not require much effort for readers to deduct that I am a Unitarian Universalist. I hope this does not get in the way or put anyone off. I certainly am not trying to convert anyone to my chosen religion. Indeed, I do not believe anyone can be converted to Unitarian Universalism; however, I do think people should be *alerted* to UUism, especially if they may have been searching for such a faith community without being aware that such a community existed.

In this little garden of literary goodies, as in most of my collections of poems, I employ a variety of styles and techniques. Although my ideas about *organic form* might seem to be particularly apt for poems about gardening, the truth is that the one poem in this book that best adheres to the concept of organic form is one that was first published in 2003 in *Songs, Scenes and Sentiments*. It rhymes pretty much when it feels like rhyming and gets along quite contentedly in free verse at other times. Some of the rhyming pieces with regular rhyme schemes I consider organic because I did not consciously plan for them to rhyme. They indicated that they wanted to rhyme, so I let them.

I do not mean to suggest here that I write in a fine frenzy or a drunken stupor or some kind of religious trance. Not at all. Writing requires real work, but like gardening, writing is a kind of work I enjoy. The old line about writing requiring 10% inspiration and 90% perspiration is no joke. If I did not enjoy helping vegetables and poems grow and develop, I'm sure I would not put forth the labor necessary to bring them to fruition.

In this volume, I experiment with some new (for me) verse forms. One of them is blank verse. I had written in free verse before, but had not tried my hand at blank verse. It's not nearly as easy as some people might think. Another new form for me is the six-line stanza called Venus and Adonis Stanza, better for me than blank verse.

As usual, some of my poems are written in that weird five-line stanza pattern which I am calling the Carroll Quintet until I learn another name for it. I can't believe I could possibly be the first or only poet to employ this stanza form.

As was the case with *Songs, and Sentiments, Grown-up's Garden* incorporates a wide variety of poetic forms and techniques as I continue my search for my own particular voice or style. I guess I may have to rely on readers to tell me what it is, as I don't know that I can identify it for myself.

Will I recognize or appreciate my own particular style if I stumble upon it? Can I be content writing poems in mainly or exclusively one style? I don't know. It might be interesting to try it.

A number of the pieces in this volume are reprinted from the earlier *Songs, Scenes and Sentiments,* sometimes without significant alterations. They were selected and republished here because of their spiritual or inspirational content. One of the selections first appeared in the Norfolk (VA) *Virginian-Pilot* daily newspaper, and several others were printed in Norfolk's *New Journal and Guide* weekly newspaper. Some pieces have appeared in regional anthologies such as *Skipping Stones, The Open Page* and *Poetry 360.*

These varied attempts to approach and discuss spirituality are a manifestation of my continuing search for meaning in life. Odd as it may seem, the search is spiritually rewarding in its own right. This unending spiritual journey rewards me with a wondrous sense of peace.

- Bill Carroll
Virginia Beach, VA

LATE-BLOOMING IDIOT

We find some poets in widely varied stages:
Some old, some young, some in their middle ages;
From youthful prodigies to ancient sages,
Their pennings pepper pages after pages.

Thus shall it be as it has ever been:
Young fledglings have been known to take the pen
And write 'till they're old women or old men,
And so we call them lifelong poets then.

Some budding geniuses write while they're young,
Then seem to write themselves out and become
Absorbed in other interests, or get stung
By other drives, new trophies to be hung.

And last,we have those wrinkled, coiled-up hoses
Whose childhood pathways lacked poetic posies;
Not budding bards, singing of wines and roses —
Late-blooming idiots: Grandma and Grandpa Moses.

Bill Carroll [Poetic Self Portrait?] (A Signature Piece)
Dedicated to society's late blooming idiots –
including the author, of course
Published in *The New Journal and Guide,* 2004

IN GREAT SHAPE FOR THE SHAPE I'M IN

People smile and ask me, "How've you been?"
I say, "In great shape for the shape I'm in."
The subject then moves on to other things
Like football or the flights of pigs with wings.

Once in a while someone will call my bluff,
Perhaps to find out if I'm full of guff;
They try to nail me with escape-proof pin
By asking, "And just what shape are you in?"

I patiently proceed then to relate
That I've survived cancer of the prostate,
Pneumonia and a lightweight heart attack
If I'd just count about a decade back.

Surprised at my quick casual medical answer,
They say, "Don't tell me you've had prostate cancer;"
Or they ask, evidently taken aback,
"You mean to say you've had a heart attack?"

I try to live each day with renewed hope,
Not bothering to worry, fret or mope
About my long-term bouts with diabetes
Or problems plaguing all Mideast peace treaties.

I'm well aware of race discrimination,
Of damage over sexual orientation
And of the seeming everlasting schisms
Resulting from ageism and sexism.

I know that tyrants still make subjects howl
And terrorists are always on the prowl,
That rich are getting richer at the cost
Of growing poverty and futures lost.

But, nonetheless, I do not lose much sleep
Sweating the promises some do not keep;
I try to join with others in the fight
To try to take *some* wrongs and make them right.

I sigh with thanks when I awake each day
And try to help some others when I may;
Indeed, we all are just life's short-term guests,
Who should feel thankful being so truly blessed.

September, 2003
(One of the "signature pieces")

DIABETIC

I have had this chronic condition
    for decades now; I have diabetes,
    but *I am not* diabetes.
I prefer to say I am diabetic
    rather than I am *a* diabetic
    (which would raise the question,
    a diabetic *what*?).
Let that word keep its adjective function;
    I don't need it as a noun.
I might die with diabetes,
    but I prefer not to die *of* diabetes
    or any of its complications.
If I am to be recalled by my Maker
    one part at a time,
    then I might go without a prostate,
    some hair, teeth, and whatever other parts
    might become defective or inoperative
    between now and then.
Meanwhile, I feel truly blessed
    to be so truly blessed (in spite of the mess).
The word *diabetic* might describe me,
    but it cannot *define* me.

Dr. Bill July, 2004
(Signature Piece)

THEIR DREAM
[A Villanelle]

They had a driving, all consuming dream:
Their family would live on its own farm.
No obstacle could throw them off the beam.

Whenever doubts cropped up and it would seem
That they might never weed out all the harm,
They had a driving, all-consuming dream.

When Tom and Sarah stepped into the stream
Of ownership, they feared no false alarm;
No obstacle could throw them off the beam.

Knowing too well the old sharecropping scheme,
With hidden traps throughout its would-be charm,
They had a driving, all-consuming dream.

They planned to let their offspring skim the cream
Of dairy, orchard, woodland, field and swarm;
No obstacle could throw them off the beam.

With steadfast faith in Power Divine, Supreme,
They purchased and passed on to us a farm;
They had a driving, all-consuming dream;
No obstacle could throw them off the beam.

This villanelle is dedicated in loving tribute to the memory
of my grandparents, Thomas Carroll, Jr. (1878-1945) and
Sarah Jones Carroll (1881-1971), who raised me from infancy.
William Carroll January, 2003
Published in *Songs, Scenes and Sentiments,* 2003
Published in *The New Journal and Guide,* 2004

THE FARM

Its purpose was to grow things: trees, livestock, grain, vegetables, some of these things grown as cash crops for market, lots of stuff grown for home use, what with lots of mouths to feed. Sure, some of Tom and Sarah's children had already left home to establish homes for themselves in towns or cities far away, but more and more, they were bringing their children to the farm — sometimes for visits, sometimes indefinitely.

So having raised lots of children of their own, the Old Folks found themselves contributing more and more to the raising of their children's children. The farm, so good at producing cash crops, foodstuffs, timber, firewood, game animals, and so many other commodities, was proving its mettle in the nurturing and growing of young human beings. Having nursed one generation of Carroll offspring to adulthood, it was repeating that process for the ensuing generation – the generation of my cousins and myself.

We grandkids constituted the current upcoming crop, growing like proverbial weeds, sometimes running wild like rampant honeysuckle or even the irrepressible kudzu. Our laughter and songs (and sometimes our cries) rebounded from the hillsides and rolled across the fertile fields as we developed from one stage to the next, always growing more capable of contributing more to the growth of the family farm.

Unbeknownst to us, as we were growing bigger and stronger, and the farm was turning out ever more revenue and nourishment, our grandparent's indebtedness was growing increasingly smaller. They had signed a contract to buy that place in 1928, before I (or even Larry or Alma) was born. My Aunts Louvinia and Sarah and my Uncle Henry were then small children. They grew up on this farm, and now we, their nieces and nephews, were tracing their well-worn footsteps. Like them, we were not born on this farm; like them, we would spend most if not all of our childhoods here.

This farm was not big by midwestern standards, nor even compared to other farms in Virginia, but to my cousins recently arrived from New York City, these sprawling acres had to look boundless. The far corner of the biggest field was half a mile from the house; a little portion of it beyond a section of outjutting woods was called Runaway Cove. Grandma said it was also called Runaway Cole in memory of an enslaved man named Cole who had escaped from that field and fled though the nearby swamps. We never heard anything about Cole's recapture, so we figured he made a clean getaway. His story certainly made interesting telling and hearing.

An even more fascinating aspect of Runaway Cove was that it was haunted! People working there would hear from the east sounds of people talking, chickens clucking, etc. although the nearest farmhouses to the east were a mile away. It was mysterious, though not frightening. Years later my scientifically oriented mind would "hypothesize" that the mile walk up and down those hills was about half that far as the crow flies, and the sounds would likely be amplified traveling across the water; if we heard the sounds of dinner bells clearly from those farms, it stood to reason that we could hear dishes rattling or babies crying if atmospheric conditions were favorable. My "scientific" explanations did nothing to dispel the magical mystery of Runaway Cove.

The farm had other features to occupy and fascinate growing children: the spring that sprang like a miniature waterfall from the side of a marl bank at the bottom of a steep ravine, the wild fruits and nuts that grew wantonly in the woods, even the snakes, hornets, skunks, and other hazardous creatures and features of the woods and fields were sources of wonder, providing endless opportunities for learning as we grew on that farm (and it grew on us). All these marvelous things were ours to use, to enjoy; by the end of the Great War we became fully aware that the farm had not belonged totally and legally to our grandparents. We learned of the official status of the farm the year Grampa died, the year Uncle Lee returned from Europe and the war.

We were then aware that Thomas and Sarah Carroll were the Real Owners of that farm after they had made the last payment which secured for them an unencumbered title to the place we called Home.

As we continued to grow in understanding, we would learn to appreciate what these two uneducated former sharecroppers, just one generation removed from slavery had done: purchased a farm in Surry County, Virginia, just fifty miles from the capitol of the Old Confederacy and paid for it between the beginning of The Great Depression and the end of The Great War.

Incredible, but true.

2002

Published in *Songs, Scenes and Sentiments,* 2003

RECONSTRUCTING THE TREE

Limbs and leaves have scattered every way:
Maryland, District, Georgia, farther away;
The fruits might not stray far from parent tree,
But still it's hard to reconstruct the tree.
We come together now from far and near,
Bringing spouses, offspring, comrades dear,
Bringing too our memories sharp or faint,
Praying for Divine help as we paint
An ever-growing picture of our past,
A portrait strong and sharp enough to last
Beyond our years to futures yet to be,
Enabling others to behold this tree:
The sturdy trunk that Tom and Sarah fed,
The roots put down by ancestors who bled
Enduring slavery's cruel, blasting pains
So later ones could make impressive gains –
And so we bring limb, branch, and twig and leaf,
Aware of their endurance through the grief;
They were survivors, showing us the way
To hang in there and seek a better day.
And now we come endowed by those of old
With strength to plan and work and reach our goal,
To bring forth richer, sweeter, better fruits,
As we dig deep and find those mighty roots.

Wm. Carroll, July, 2002, Carroll Family Reunion, Williamsburg, VA
In *Songs, Scenes, Sentiments,* 2003; *New Journal & Guide,* 2004

NOW IS THE TIME

We look forward to success,
Ultimate happiness,
As existing somewhere just around the bend;
We should not have to wait
To sing and celebrate
Until we've reached some great and glorious END.

Each day provides the chance
To triumph and to dance,
To revel in a moment at the top;
We need not wait and look
For closing of life's book
To bring our earthly progress to a STOP.

True happiness and pride
Reside within the ride,
Each step and stop a chance for jubilation;
So always look for how
To enjoy eternal Now:
Success in JOURNEY, NOT in DESTINATION.

Wm. Carroll, July, 2003 (For the Williamsburg Carrolls)
To my Cousin Arlene M. Carroll and her sisters and all
their children, grandchildren, great-grand... etc.
Pass it on.

SOWING SEEDS TO SUCCEED

("The Garden Sonnet")

A serious gardener, I like to think that I
    Have faith enough to trust in Power Divine
To bring a fruitful end to most of my
    Attempts to grow a veggie, tree or vine.

Likewise, I tell myself that through my years
    Of teaching, writing, mentoring and speaking,
I have assisted persons, lives, careers,
    And helped some students reach some goals worth
    seeking.

I plant the seed with hope that it will grow,
    Producing fruit that's wonderful to see;
I plant with faith, and faithfully I know
    The sweetest fruit is called Sweet Charity.

The harvest that comes forth from class or sod
    Is all the proof I need that there's a God.

Bill Carroll, April, 2003
Published in the Norfolk *Virginian-Pilot,* September, 2003
Published in the (Norfolk) *New Journal and Guide,* 2004

THE BLISS OF GROWTH

To watch as things grow can provide us a lifetime
      of pleasure;
To help plants to grow can bring blessings beyond
      any measure;
Helping frail, tender young plants to emerge from
      the sod
Gives a feeling of power and burgeoning kinship
      with God.

But plants are not all that need nurture and
      kindhearted sharing;
Most living things bask in that warmth that we all
      share in caring,
Responding with growth spurts or maybe a
      startling new start
In gratitude for that assistance that flows heart to
      heart.

No one can do everything; that's undeniably
      true,
But everyone can help with something, and that
      includes you.
We all can extend to some poor struggling
      creature a hand
And give our own gifts to help grow Mother
      Nature's Grand Plan.

2003 – Published in *The New Journal and Guide*

THE SPIRAL OF LIFE

Onward and upward must be the natural route for us; our
organs of sight, hearing, and smelling are all located
in our heads, at or near the top of the body, not lower
down with other organs which have important
functions, but do not indicate the direction we should
travel through life.

God did not put eyes in the back of humans' heads (as a
possible indication that we should move backwards);
eyes situated in the feet could signify downward
movement, but our eyes are in our heads, in the front
of the head; what more evidence do we need to tell us
to be moving on up?

Some might say our life's path is a circle, that we always
come back to the point from which we started, but if
that were truly accurate, we would be repeating the
same experiences with no variations, no progress;
these seeming circles must be more like the threads
of a screw.

Our every turn should take us ever higher as we drill and
probe ever deeper into the mysteries we encounter;
we should seek to scale the peaks because they are
there, and if we have not experienced the heights and
plumbed their profound secrets, that should be all the
incentive we need to keep climbing, striving,
reaching, growing.

Seedlings and sunflowers reach for life-giving light
instinctively; can't we humans use our God-given
minds to do likewise? Should we not be striving ever
onward and upward toward the best that we can be
and the best that we can give? Isn't this the way to
fulfill our divine mission?

2003
Published in *The New Journal and Guide,* 2004

A TREE GROWS IN VA BEACH
(And Everywhere Else)

A

tree

labeled as

Bradford Pear

is truly beautiful, even in

the winter when leafless and gray,

even without the white or growing greens

or fiery oranges and reds of other seasons, the

tree still keeps that classic ace-of-spades shape

without the aid of pruning or binding. We see them

arrayed along the medians of streets and highways of

cities, towns and countryside. They grow like yeast. Ah,

there's the rub. The faster they grow, the more likely they

are to split and to let that split-off part come crashing and

smashing down on whatever unfortunate animals, vegetables

or minerals might happen to be under them. To the east of

my veggie garden, Mike and Carolyn had a pair of these twin

beauties in their yard until a stormy sister named Isabel sent

split off splitfalls from those erstwhile beauties into the edge

of my garden. Well, better my garden than their house. My

next-door neighbor had one of four pieces split from his

tree hit his house, doing only minimal damage. These

trees actually bear fruit, but not even the birds seem

to like it. The main

fruit seems to be its

own destruction.

September, 2003

15

CROSSING THE CHESAPEAKE

I

The night is dark and silky like a sleek, expensive evening
gown as the greyhound prowls down the long slender
neck of Delmarva; reaching down from the neck, a
magnificent string of iridescent pearls plunges into
the mysterious night, perhaps seeking to connect that
elegant neck to the warm, sensuously seductive body
of the voluptuous vixen called Virginia.

Nearly twenty miles of bridges and tunnels lie ahead, an
awesome wonder of the modern technological world;
the misty rain sweeps stealthily through the eerie
night, adding a shimmer to the pearls as we approach
and pass under them one by one, the road surface
giving us a magic carpet ride touching past and
possibly future.

II

In the storied past of this region (so proud of its history),
slave ships plied the waters of these firths and sounds
and roads, bringing human cargo stolen, bought or
hood-winked from Africa to then unknown and
uniquely inhumane living(?) conditions when
purchased and dispersed from Jamestown, Norfolk,
Richmond, other ports.

The brawn and brains of these restrained and fettered ones
        made possible the progress of the fledgling nation,
        made unacknowledged and largely unknown
        contributions to Richmond, Washington,
        development of the Great West, and yes, even such
        worldly wonders as this system of bridges and
        tunnels.

III

And now, more than a century after the abolition of the
        "peculiar Institution," we descendants of debased and
        degraded but not destroyed progenitors ride the
        hurrying hound down the magically mysterious night,
        being carried back to Old Virginny, Virgin State and
        Mother of Presidents, land of contradictions, proud of
        her history while disowning unflattering parts of it.

The beauty of the mist-enshrin´ed night that makes a pearly
        necklace of the bridge lights cannot camouflage nor
        cancel out those half-truths lurking behind its beauty;
        Yes, Virginia is a big tourist destination with
        attractions natural and man-made, a great place to
        visit, a good place to reside – mountains, beaches, or
        in between; but dark shadows haunt her history like
        phantoms rising from the Great Dismal Swamp.

Earlier versions published in
Songs, Scenes and Sentiments, 2003 and *Skipping Stones,* 2005

ON KWANZAA

"You celebrate Kwanzaa?" they asked, seeing my kufi
and Afrocentric jewelry. I said "Yes," pleased with their
awareness of Kwanzaa. "So you don't celebrate Christmas."
I insisted that I did observe the Christian holiday. They held
that those celebrating Kwanzaa did not observe Christmas. I
said I probably knew more people who celebrated Kwanzaa
than they did and that all of them celebrated Christmas also.
I told them Kwanzaa was a cultural observance, not a ritual
of religion, that the observances need not be mutually ex-
clusive, that folks of any (or no) religious belief could
partake in the rituals of Kwanzaa, that this cultural
holiday was born in *America*, using ideas and ideals
from many African cultures, that the holiday was
being celebrated in many parts of the African
diaspora by Christians and non-Christians
alike. Most students agreed that people
could take part in this holiday with-
out changing or losing faith, that
broadening our cultural hori-
zons need not diminish
our appreciation of
Jesus or Martin
King or any-
one or any-
thing else.

Bill Carroll – 2002-06
Earlier version published in *Songs, Scenes and Sentiments*, 2003

UHURU

Freedom's not just another word for
       nothing left to do;
True, Janis might have sung it,
       but that did not make it true.
The drive to end oppression
       drove oppressed people to screw
Their courage to the sticking point,
       so that they overthrew
The powerful cowards who could make
       their lives a hellish stew.

A little Kiswahili word
       can sum it up for you:
It can supply a rallying cry
       for distressed people who
Have had their fill of slavery's ill
       and now are ready to
Make heartfelt vow for Freedom Now
       to last a lifetime through,
To live and be perpetually free
       like falcons soaring through the blue.

That little Kiswahili word
        can sound around the ocean blue,
Or certainly ring true for those
        who've suffered greatly through
The lasting pangs imposed by gangs
        of spirit robbers who
Would try to part spirit from heart
        of people strong and true
Who do hold out and bravely shout
        that mighty word, UHURU!

March, 2003
Dedicated to the spirit of oppressed people who have gained freedom and
also to those working toward it.
Published in *The New Journal and Guide,* 2004
and in *Skipping Stones, 2005*

DRUM CALL

[to be spoken rhythmically like the beating of a tom-tom or djembe]

When I hear those powerful drumbeats that say "Africa,"
The soul deep inside me responds to the pull of the call;
Those heart-pounding rhythms that span the wide global
     diaspora
Find "welcome home" signs in the wide open hearts of us
     all.

The notion that black folks have rhythm's become
     stereotypical,
But stereotypes tend to develop in part out of facts;
Descendants of Europe clap hands in a manner that's
     rhythmical,
But often will struggle with offbeat and back beat attacks.

For scions of Africa living here in North America,
The rhythms stay strong in our growing identity search;
Tho drums were outlawed among us in those old English
     colonies,
We still banged out makeshift percussion as we sang in
     church.

The drum in the homeland provided a means of community,
Accompanied dances, helped people to communicate;
Those rhythms can still give diverse folk a real sense of unity
And build bridges over the widening chasms of hate.

2002

REMEMBERING 9/11

Two years later, I can think of it a bit more calmly; two years
    ago, I was in my truck headed for my vegetable garden,
    listening to Sports Squawk Radio — regular
    programming interrupted to talk about airliners crashing
    into NY skyscrapers, into the Pentagon in Northern VA,
    into an empty farm field in rural PA.

At home watching TV, seeing endlessly repeated reruns of
    the nightmare footage: the second plane hitting the
    second tower, buildings falling, people running
    screaming, all the garish trappings of a badly made
    horror movie — or the scarier horror of a nightmare
    from which we could not awaken.

In September of 2002, I wrote a letter to my Cousin Silvia
    (Li'l Sissy) saying that the significance of 9/11 for me
    was that it was her birthday; I hope the letter was as
    soothing for her as writing it was for me; thinking of
    what a blessing she was to her brothers and to others
    served to counter the bad vibes still emanating from
    those scenes.

I have since been to New York City, ridden past Ground
    Zero, talked with acquaintances of victims or survivors
    of that double inferno, made modest contributions to
    efforts to clean up and restore the site; this year, with
    Taliban still rampant and hatred of America still strong,
    the peace that has found my life is not likely to be
    shaken by any of man's inhumanity.

Dr. Bill — 2003

THE BEACON

Bea-con n. Something that warns or guides.
v. to provide with or serve as a beacon.

Unitarian Universalism has Beacon Book Publishers. UU
Association headquarters is on Beacon Street in Boston.
Historically salient beacons dot the coastline of our
Atlantic shores, casting guiding beams and ship-saving
rays into the nighttime bleakness.

Another special beacon sheds its rays from jagged East Coast
to rugged West Coast and all over our multicultural
continent, discovering and illuminating GEMs, which
circumstances may have hidden in poverty, ignorance
and grime.

Whether in Mid-Atlantic Virginia, subtropical Florida, deep
in the heartland of Indiana, or any place on *terra firma*,
this Beacon is like the biblical city on the hill, whose
light cannot be hidden, whose wealth is always shared.

The Beacon lights the way as a pioneer, leader, mentor,
benefactor – generating hope and motivating others to
emulate him, daring the more daring followers to exceed
him;

The Beacon guides and leads, knowing not how far his light
shines.

October, 2003
Inspired by and dedicated to Howard G. Adams, Ph. D.

PREVENTABLE EPIDEMIC?

Yes, education is the remedy
>To cure the malady called ignorance;
But hatred and deep-seated bigotry
>Can build rock-hard impregnable defense
Against known facts as mighty as the sea.

So racism and fears of difference,
>And festering, phobic longtime bigotry
Surround the hater with a shield that's dense
>Enough to render vain the pounding sea,
Breaking in vain against the rocks of ignorance.

Education grows vast like the ocean,
>With ideas coming in on every tide;
Facts and attitudes, even emotions
>Expand and swell, becoming deep and wide;
But bigotry arrests all growth, all motion.

Therefore, it behooves the School of Light
>To shine its beacon beams upon the youth,
And teach them to seek out the good and right,
>To explore various routes toward the truth
That makes us free to fight the righteous fight.

Dr. Bill – March, 2002
Inspired by and dedicated to the youth (especially
Adam Smith of the Unitarian Church of Norfolk,
Unitarian Universalist)
Published in *Songs, Scenes and Sentiments,* 2003
and in *The New Journal and Guide,* 2004

THE HEART'S TRUE COLORS

African hosts to a loved and respected European guest:
"You may have a white face, but your heart is black."

1954, a landmark year,
      The year of the Brown Decision:
      "No more segregation in public education,"
      The year of my high school graduation.
      My heart was young and hopeful,
            But already made skittish by the realities of
            living in the American South at mid-century.

Had some seer or soothsayer said to me in 1954,
      "Forty years down life's road
      Twice as many white visages will visit
      Your hospital room as black ones,"
      My response would have been succinct
      and snappy, but sportingly sincere:
            "You have got to be crazier than a loud-
            mouthed, Brooklyn-dwelling Yankee fan!"

1994, a momentous year indeed,
      Children grown and on their own,
      Wife an attorney, my hair almost gone.
      My heart was now older, and the old ticker
      Was not in the pink and still growing sicker:
      Clogged with cholesterol, dogged by diabetes,
      Pressured by job stress and high-level entreaties.
      Chest pain! — Hospital! — Angioplasty!

Not really a close-to-death experience, but
merely a scared-half-to-death experience. Not
Fred Sanford's "Big One," but then all heart
attacks are as serious as — well, you know.

A week later, home again, resting,
    Holding cat, watching cartoons, reading books,
    writing notes of thanks to those who called, sent
    cards, books, flowers or live plants —
    Those who came in and tried to cheer me.
    The score was plain with their addresses near me:
        For every black visitor, two others were white.
        How could this friendship scoreboard be right?

Years later, assessing this bounteous blessing:
    My heart had to learn for the sake of its health
    That real love is really invaluable wealth.
    Hearts are not rated by color or size;
    A matter like color of skin, hair or eyes
    Bears no relation to goodness or rightness;
    Love's not a matter of blackness or whiteness.
    Neither brownness, redness, nor any shade of tan
    Determines the heart of a woman, child or man.
    Those who love me and my significant others
        Are truly my spiritual sisters and brothers.
        Blessed are they who in times of great strife
        Share love, for their hearts are truly the color of
        life.

2001 — Dedicated to the Reverend Judith Morris
Published in *Songs, Scenes and Sentiments,* 2003

NEW LIFE MAKES LIFE NEW

It's easy to see why countless myths
        in endless times and boundless climes
Have come to us regarding the unrelenting
        return of spring each year,
After the long, dark, cold, scary, dead-
        looking days of winter time
Have filled frail folks' hearts with dread
        and ever-growing fear
That heat and light might not return
        despite the sun's late-winter climb.

The flowers, trees and woodland creatures
        are all attuned to Nature's master plan;
Not so some of the humans who
        consider themselves to be so smart
That they can conquer Nature
        instead of being content to understand
That we and they should gladly play
        our vital, integral part,
To take our rightful place in the continu-
        ing cycle of the Great Grand Plan.

Each year, the ever-cycling, never-failing,
        sure return of spring
Brings to us the spirit of rebirth,
        resurrection, real triumph of Life
Over darkness, death, destruction,
        demon, the dreaded thing
That threatens our existence with vain fears
        of vast, unconquerable strife
And tries to make us give up hope
        and see Life as a fleeting fling.

Whether we be human, wild beast,
           tree or fish, bird or April flower,
The message of Love and Life is there,
           written clear and true for all to see;
Ever springing Life is all around
           to show to us its awesome power;
We celebrate with lilies, eggs, bunnies,
           lambs, the Cross of Calvary,
And other symbols of Life's triumph
           as seen in rainbow and in April shower.

For human creatures the most impressive
           message of the spring may be
A sign of life with a personal message,
           particularly close and clear;
A family is reshaped when parents
           welcome home a brand-new baby,
And Only Son is now Big Brother
           to the baby, sister-soft and dear;
Life is renewed and reshaped with
           the advent of the family's new baby.

May, 2003 – For the Danny R. Reed Family,
especially for Ms. Harper Elizabeth Reed, born April, 2003

ALL-CONQUERING LOVE

To hearts in love, all colors are sublime:
The eyes of love see not the bounds of time,
Religion, culture, nationality;
Real love can conquer rationality.
Some people might say, "Leave that person! Run!
Run far away and be with your own kind."
But love responds: "I'm neither mad nor blind;
I follow laws unfettered by false rules
Enacted by provincial, narrow fools."
All seasons bestow beauty on the year;
Both night and day can fill our hearts with cheer.
If man-made notes from ebony and ivory
Can serenade us with sweet sounds of harmony,
Perhaps there is a lesson there for you and me:
To grow our lives to create larger melody.
Villainous veils of fear and hate and doubt
May try to build strong walls to keep some out;
But Love gives us the strength and will to win,
And weaves wide webs, welcoming US ALL IN.

Bill Carroll, Ph. D. — December, 2002
For the wedding of Tony Bly and Donna Gerych, 12/21/02

UNQUENCHABLE FIRES

In olden days at Christmas time
    A yule log was the rule;
It kept its light and warmed the nights
    Throughout the weeks of yule.
In every age and every clime,
    In every vogue and fashion,
All creatures feel the strong appeal
    Fanned by the fires of passion.
When those fires meld with fondness held
    Within the hearts of lovers,
The bond that grows and binds them close
    Can last beyond all others.
Those fires that burn when hair has turned
    To show maturity's gray
Are true love's sign, the lasting kind,
    The love that's here to stay.

Bill and Thelma Carroll
July-August, 2002
For the wedding of Louise Dabney Stokes
and Robert Cosby — 8/3/02

GREG AND I

We are both Capricorns – birthdays sometimes
        overshadowed by nearby holidays: his birthday in
        late December, mine in early January.

Loving to write, we have had literary productions inspired by
        potentially life-threatening medical situations:

His brain tumor led him to write a series of letters which
        eventually became the book, "Magic and Loss,"
        dedicated to his daughter, Emily;

My heart attack and the resultant telling and retelling of the
        story of how I became aware of having so many
        Caucasian friends led to the writing of one of my
        favorite poems, "The Heart's True Colors."

We have made joyful noises together in various combos as
        well as in the church choir; he usually sings first bass,
        occasionally second bass, and sometimes even tenor -
        – has been assigned choral solo parts on occasion; I
        sing second bass, have sung first, rarely attempted
        tenor, have shared a couple of choral solo parts in
        about eighteen years in choir.

Not great readers of music, we enjoy making instrumental
        music (anyhow); he does wonderful work on guitar
        or piano with songs that are comfortably familiar to
        him; I generally stick safely to percussion
        instruments (tambourine, claves, various drums, etc.),
        rarely risking a venture into the realm of guitar or
        piano.

In one of our combo performances, I found myself playing
        guitar while Greg was whaling away on tambourine. I
        had to ask myself, "What is wrong with this picture?"
        Oh well, in the world which Greg and I share, we
        may not always be interchangeable, but we are
        always harmoniously compatible.

Bill Carroll, 2003
For my friend, Greg Raver-Lampman

GOOD GARDENS MAKE GOOD NEIGHBORS

It was more than twenty years after the late John L. Fisk and
     I had met; I had tended vegetable gardens in various
     locations on his still expansive, though shrinking,
     acres; and one year he and I had jointly planted and
     harvested a not so successful crop of Hayman sweet
     potatoes, my only attempt at raising them.

I always shared veggies with members of the Fisk family as
     well as with the renters who lived in Mrs. Fisk's
     properties and with many of her neighbors and also
     with friends in my own neighborhood a couple of
     miles distant.

In 1999 my garden was right smack in the yard of Widow
     Helen Fisk; it was mid-June, and I was scurrying to
     get to the opening of Sheri's 1999 celebration of
     Juneteenth in Hampton Roads; my illness began that
     day, though I paid it little mind.

I was soon too sick to ignore it any longer: blood sugar
     soaring, appetite waning almost to the vanishing
     point; when The Wife and I went to Dr. Brooks, he
     sent me straight to the hospital, dehydrated, yet weak
     as an overly-watered cheap cocktail.

This hospitalization marked the sickest period I had ever
     known; I had pneumonia, with some of the infection
     tap-dancing on or near my diaphragm, triggering the
     hiccup reflex, gifting me with uncontrollable hiccups
     at any time — always inconvenient and usually
     unexpected.

In addition to the hiccuping, I did a lot of vomiting, which
succeeded in keeping me dehydrated despite the IVs
and all; the nausea was so bad that I shared my bed
with a plastic container which I affectionately dubbed
The Barf Barge.

Meanwhile, back on Avalon Avenue, garden neighbors were
concerned: "Where's Bill?" "What's happened to
Bill?" "Is he sick?" On Saturday, my wife informed
Bobbi, one of Mrs. Fisk's tenants, that I was in
hospital, and Bobbi told her to return at 5:00 that
evening.

Now, my Sweetie is no gardener, but she knows I love
gardening, and she loves me, so although she had (at
best) a scant idea of what I was talking about when I
told her what needed doing in the garden, when she
told Bobbi, the Fisks, and several neighbors, they did
it.

When Sweetie told me about the "garden party for Dr. Bill,"
my spirits were elevated, lifting my body in the
process; nausea ceased, hiccups abated, blood sugar
controlled. (IV and antibiotics continued still.).

When I pictured the Langhornes training the cucumbers up
the bean fence, Sweetie and Susan spreading straw
among the melons, Ira and Bobbi digging out wire
grass and nut grass, and Queen Helen herself digging
potatoes, I knew my wife was not the only one there
who loved me.

September, 2003
Dedicated to Mrs. Helen Fisk

34

APPRECIATE THE ANGELS

A man climbed a high tree during a flood
 And prayed to God to save him from the storm,
The rising water and the choking mud,
 Which he knew well could do him fatal harm;
And God told him that He would send a friend
To save him from a bitter, watery end.

A motorboat soon came along, and men
 Then offered him a ride to a safe place;
He thanked them kindly, but did promptly send
 Them on their way while waiting for God's grace;
The same thing happened when a copter crew
Let down a ladder, but he spurned that too.

He drowned in the flood waters, and when he
 Did face his Maker, he was somewhat miffed
And said, "You promised, Lord, that you'd save me;"
 His Lord said, "I won't make you take a gift;
You had the chance for boat or chopper flight
But chose to stay and not leave, come what might."

Do we expect an angel to have wings,
 To carry flaming sword or golden harp?
"Touched by an Angel" gave us this great thing:
 To perceive angels, we need to look sharp –
Not for a halo or some flaming brand,
But fellow creatures, lending us a hand.

An angel can be whoever will give
 Assistance when we have a dire need,
Perhaps just to sustain the will to live
 Or courage to attempt a valiant deed;

We need to recognize our angels and
Be thankful for that heavenly helping hand.

The angel could be your own faithful spouse,
    A parent, sibling, or a loving friend,
A friendly stranger dashing to your house
    To bring a fledgling fire to an end
Before that flame can grow to monstrous zone
And make an ashy memory of your home.

The trooper who shows up the moment that
    We need a helping hand along the road
To help us change a most untimely flat
    Or redistribute an ungainly load;
The paramedic, the deft cleanup crew —
They're angels all with vital tasks to do.

Angels can come in many shapes and sizes,
    Exhibit diverse shapes and varied hues;
They may sometimes employ clever disguises,
    So that we might not have the chance to use
An option or employ our latitude
To offer them our thanks or gratitude.

If life sometimes seems burdensome and rife
    With troubles, angels come to help us out,
To help alleviate the pains of life,
    Just when we fear that we will lose the bout;
The way to show our thanks for kindness done
Is — pass it on to yet another one.

September, 2003, revised 2006
A version appeared in *The New Journal and Guide* in 2004.

LITTLE BIG MAN ON CAMPUS

Standing on Wright Avenue near the juncture of the twin
college towns, I felt (and probably looked) just as lost
as I actually was. Spotting a campus building with an
information counter, I strode over there and asked the
two young ladies if they knew anything about a
student dramatic production scheduled for that
weekend.

The white coed asked if it would be in the Krannart Center. I
had no idea what the Krannart Center was, but
thought it sounded way too fancy to be a venue for
my kid's play. The cute black undergrad said simply,
"Bill Carroll?"

I successfully refrained from jumping over the counter and
hugging her as I explained that I was Bill's father,
there to see the play, and totally unfamiliar with the
U of I campus. My lack of familiarity with the
campus and the towns began sloughing off like
superfluous fur from a shedding feline as I grew
familiar with key parts of the massive campus and the
rather unmassive towns of Champaign and Urbana.

I learned that Bill worked in a restaurant on the Champaign
side of the Ungreat Divide, but resided on the Urbana
side. In the restaurant, I told the manager who I was
and where I was from, asked if my son could have
the afternoon off to be with me. "Oh no! we can't
operate the place without him; you'll have to wait
until his regular quitting time."

Turns out that my son did practically everything in the place at one time or another: cooking, waiting tables, cleaning floors, running the register, whatever needed doing at that time. Well, as far as I knew, his previous restaurant experiences occurred in one summer gig at a Taco Bell in Virginia Beach. The kid had obviously acquired a talent for making himself indispensable.

He was a big man at the restaurant. I would learn that he was also a surprisingly big man on campus as well. The only thing I knew about the play I had flown halfway across a continent to see was that it was entitled "A House Divided" (and that my son and heir was its author). The show turned out to be much more than I had been led to expect.

Since it was a student production, I didn't know if it would be in a classroom, a basement, or what. It was not in the ultramodern Krannart Center, but in a lovely auditorium about a century old; at night, with its lights on, it was a gigantic jewel box. I attended two performances, a matinee for family audiences and a nighttime show for a "mature" crowd. I saw precious little difference.

Those students had cleverly combined music, dance, and drama in a stunning showcase that incorporated works by known authors interspersed with original works by Bill, Terry, and other members of their MPAACT theatre troupe. The centerpiece was Bill's play whose full title was "A House Divided Remains Oppressed." It dealt with intra-racial color prejudice. Well written, well directed, well staged, well performed. Reggie's mom was even more impressed than I was. She had not been pleased with the previous year's presentation.

It was at the party following the play that I learned what a
truly big man my son had become on the campus. It
seemed that every black undergrad at U of I knew
Bill, and the white ones who wanted to be considered
hip just had to know him too or risk the stigma of
unhipness.

My son was barely 5' 9", and even with his beautiful biceps,
proud pecs, and awesome abs, he could hardly
contest the impressive bulk of Reggie or even the
studly stature of Carl, for that matter. Yet, there was
no doubt that he was a big man in the creation and
presentation of the theatre production, and on the
dance floor at the party, as well as in the restaurant.

I could be particularly proud to be his Pop, even if the
"bouncer" at the party tried to bar me – and Reggie's
girlfriend – from the festivities despite our emotional
proximity to two of the principals.

I could recall enjoying something of the status of BMOC as
an undergrad, and Bill probably could too, but here
he was in grad school being lionized in a way I could
only catch on the rebound.

2003
For my son, William S. Carroll, of whom I am
extremely and justifiably proud.

EVELYN HELLINGER

(1921-2003)

I feel somewhat deprived now that she's gone,
Not just because she died, tho death was quick;
She'd lived a lively, full eighty-two years
Before succumbing to a short sick spell.
I do regret not knowing her as well –
As well I might have in near three decades;
I knew her husband, her beloved Joey
A longer time, as we both worked at State;
I later learned she was employed at both
The campuses of NSU and ODU.
They both were left-wing social activists
Whose words and actions left some lasting marks
Upon Virginia's rightward leaning stance;
The city, region, and the Commonwealth
Are changed forever, thanks in part to them.
Late in her life, I learned that she and I
Were both enamored with our growing plants;
She actually became a master gardener,
While I just gardened sans the formal tag.
A year before her death she gave to me
A plant completely new to my survey
Called Japanese Parilla, a red herb
Especially useful in salads, and
Potentially useful in soups as well.

This new red plant now thrives among my herbs;
I understand it's an aggressive soul,
Not altogether unlike its great donor;
I plan to keep it under some control
And watch it flourish, raising Evelyn's honor.

In tribute, 2003

GARDENING VS GARDENING

I heard their talk of gardening, and I,
As I approached some ladies in the church,
Was full aware that they were speaking of
The care and feeding of attractive plants
Like flowers, shrubbery, perhaps small trees.

Like a child who knows he should keep silent, I
Did clear my throat as I stepped up and said,
"I will admit I'm fond of flowers and shrubs,
But in my land, a garden brings forth food;
Flowers and shrubs are merely landscape plants."

Linda, like a lawyer at rebuttal,
Assayed my comment before giving hers:
A knockout counterstroke to leave me mute —
With pretty face and manner most disarming,
She firmly said, "What you do is called FARMING."

2003

SPRINGTIME'S GREEN – AND RED

Vine-clad fence in springtime's morning light
Reveals the fence's vines and peas, bright green;
Upon the fence sits cardinal, blaze-red bright —
An artist's or photographer's dream scene;
On closer look, my gardener's keen eye sees,
That pretty bird is EATING my green peas!

Bill Carroll, March, 2005

AS TIME PASSES

As time goes past, so too do lots of us,
     We part as friends and go our separate ways;
We leave by car, by train or plane or bus,
     But time keeps speeding toward our final days;
We need to keep contact with old-time friends
Before the chance for earthly contact ends.

We need to let our friends know of our love
     And that we care what's happening to them;
We need to share communications of
     Events that gleam for us as precious gems;
For joy that's shared is joy that is compounded,
As sorrow shared is sorrow soon confounded.

What if our hair has turned all gray or white,
     Or even if it's turned completely loose?
If brain within the head still has insight,
     And body parts have not lost every use,
We have a duty to do what we can
To reach to others our still helpful hands.

So if it seems that life has frightening omens
     That make us wonder if we've lost the way,
And life flows like a stream of senior moments
     Confusing us about the hour and day,
We still can raise what voice we have in praise
And still share blessings in our golden days.

2003
William "Doc" Carroll (Class of '54)
For all the alumni of Surry County Training School and
Luther P. Jackson High School, especially the class of 1954
Presented July 31, 2004

EVADING ISABEL

We knew before it came: "Evacuate!"
We did not wish to risk the kind of mayhem
Which could result from a Hurricane Cat 4;
A Category 3 against the shores
Of Carolina's Outer Banks could make
Virginia Beach a deep, downed-tree-strewn swamp.
We boarded up the house and hit the road
Before majority of VaBeach crowd
Although we did encounter quite a few
OBX refugees bound north and west;
We landed in the City of The Star,
The hub of Roanoke Valley and the West
Of Old Dominion's multi-landed state.
While there, we met folks who'd arrived from
Smithfield,
From Chesapeake, and certainly, from the Beach;
We shared congratulations having fled
The threats of Isabel by going west;
While in those hills, we learned some local lore
And visited the shrine of Booker T.
Returning showed us growing scenes of dread,
Of downed trees over power lines and roads,
Of outages that stretched from Appomatox
To Suffolk without signs of that mysterious
Power we tend to take for granted till
We do not have it and are then bereft
Of means to warm or heat and feed us
In manner to which we've become accustomed.

    Rough thrown-together crews of personnel
Worked ant-like to clear lanes for motorists
To make their snail paced way along the road
That's designated US 460;
On many properties along the way,
Multiple trees had fallen in the yards;
The miracle of these dramatic scenes
Was that so many times the family's home
Was left unscathed, unharmed by any trees.
    We'd heard from Neighbor Bob while in Blackstone
That our home was not damaged by the storm,
Although Bob's own house got a light caress
From part of the tree in his yard which split
In four parts, largest of the four still leaning
Against his garage and parts of his roof.
Although our neighborhood was without juice,
It came back on within a few hours' time.
The food left in our freezer had not thawed.
    Enumerating blessings ruled the day
As we took stock of our blessed situation;
Some folks might say we wasted time and cash
By pulling out from our own sanctuary,
But we do not regret the choices made,
And would repeat them if there seemed a need.

October, 2003

LIFE'S LONGING AFTER ITSELF

In the slowly ebbing but still lasting wake of Hurricane
    Isabel, crabapple trees and Bradford pear trees
    blooming off season; Is it because the autumn weather
    is so balmy? No. We frequently have soothingly mild
    autumns, so the trees are blooming because somehow
    somewhere deep within the pith and foundational fiber
    of their being, they feel a threat from the hurricane, a
    threat which has not gone north through Canada, nor
    blown harmlessly out into the North Atlantic. The
    unseasonable white flecks among what's left of the
    green foliage, which should be ready to don colorful
    fall garb, are a manifestation of the inborn urge of
    living things to perpetuate their own kind.
If you or I were in a comatose state, our very cells and
    tissues would fight for whatever semblance of life was
    extant without a conscious brain to tell them so. The
    first law of nature is self-preservation; not far behind is
    reproduction of the species. Is this why sex is such a
    big deal in various societies – even if some of them
    treat it in widely differing ways? For some, sex is
    much more for recreation than for re-creation, but so
    what? Even recreational copulators know where babies
    come from and have learned well the lessons of the
    birds and bees. If sex were not such a fun activity,
    would animal life cease to exist? Do plants and even
    one-celled creatures *enjoy* reproduction? Just
    wondering.

Dr. Bill – October, 2003

WORKS OF GOD

"Be quiet; don't you know God's doing His work?"
     Our grandmother would say during a storm;
I had my doubts, but was not such a jerk
     To put them into words that might do harm;
Was God not working on a sunny day,
Or when sweet flowers wafted on our way?

In high school I learned that insurance firms
     Called natural disasters "Acts of God;"
I deemed this a most unjust sack of worms,
     To wrap bad news in some convenient pod
Which blamed the Deity for matters bad
While ignoring those that make us glad.

If we blame the Creator for bad things,
     Why can't we give some balance to the scale,
Give thanks for happenings that make us sing
     Or gladden our hearts within this lowly vale?
Why don't we call our lives or a loved one's face
A "Work of God," a gift of Divine Grace?

2003
Published in *The New Journal and Guide,* 2004

ROSES IN WINTERTIME

Even their Latin name is pretty: *Camellia Japonica.* When the mornings are getting crisp like skins of super-baked sweet potatoes, and the nights are calling for blankets and rising thermostats, colorful varieties of *Camellia Sassanqua* will burst boldly into bloom, but most of what I call *real camellias* will wait until days are windy and frigid before making their spectacular impact and imprint upon the wintry landscape, some of them waiting until the crocuses and daffodils are announcing the advent of spring.

We could do well to learn from these spectacular seasonal showstoppers that give such welcome color to dreary yards, as they stand with their cotton-candy red, pink, white or speckle-spotted faces adorning deep-green foliage in the dead of winter. When nights are long and dark, and days are dank and dreary, why don't we brighten up each other's existence, not just with our looks, but with our colorfully bright attitudes and deeds?

December, 2003

FLAG WAIVERS

Without a doubt, they think they are among
The utmost patriots who've ever sung
The nation-praising songs and shared the stories
Of heroism and consummate glories.

They fly Old Glory through the storms and rains;
Though this is flag abuse, they take no pains
To properly illuminate at night
The Stars and Stripes' nocturnal ghostly flight.

Some use vehicles to abuse their flags,
Allowing weather to reduce to rags
Those formerly bright colorful old banners —
A certain sign of absence of flag manners.

Those ragged ensigns should be quietly burned,
As troops and scouts have dutifully learned;
But self-styled super patriots usually turn
Against those who suggest a flag should burn.

Though no one doubts a boy scout or marine
Is patriotic as a blade is keen,
They burn old flags as part of protocol,
And no one seems to deem this wrong at all.

Therefore, it must not be the actual burning
That sets those super patriots' innards churning,
But rather the implied symbolic speech
That makes the *waivers* rant and howl and screech.

I hear no protests from flag waivers when
The flag is flaunted by auto salesmen;
They do not fuss if pols on either wing
Enfold themselves in flags to do their thing.

Flag wavers who waiver over burning flags
While flying from their cars disgusting rags
Just might do well to make some effort learning
That flags can suffer far worse fate than burning.

2003

SHARING THE BOUNTY

Activity which gardeners enjoy more
Than giving free food to the needy and greedy
Is giving free advice to all who want it;
Not many people want gardening advice,
So veggie growers just resolve to share
The foodstuffs grown, no fear of lack of takers.

I take great pleasure in the heaps of food
I give the local food bank every year:
Tomatoes, potatoes (the white and the sweet),
Cucumbers, carrots, squash (summer and winter),
Corn, watermelons, other melons (different
Muskmelons in different years; I'm always learning),
Beans (limas, snaps, and others), and so forth.

Some crops have not developed to the point
To have enough to share with the food bank;
Some others I just raise enough to eat
Or give to friendly folks who live nearby;
I hope to have more berries coming in
To share with other folks, not just the birds:
My strawberries, blackberries, wineberries
And blueberries might have a bountiful future
If guarded from birds and slugs and other pests.

Persistent perennials like asparagus and artichokes,
Though perched atop the alphabet, are slow to grow
To where their scanty fruits can be be liberally shared;
Although I am aging, I plant for the dimly seen future;
This gives me ever more reason to look forward —
As if I needed increased motivation to live.

Dr. Bill – 2003
(A Signature Piece)

CAN'T HAVE A MESSAGE WITHOUT A MESS

[Advice to would-be writers]

It takes super-tart, jaw-locking lemons to make good
lemonade, REAL lemonade; the sours and sweets
complement (and maybe compliment) each other in
essential ways. At age 5, my son said he liked stories
with good endings and bad middles (out of the
mouths of kindergarten kids!). My son knew that the
bad middle enhanced the goodness of the good end.

If life throws you a curve, Adjust Your Swing! Some people
say, "I know I've got a story; I just don't have time to
write." Everybody has the same 24 hours in every
day. Writing requires discipline. This discipline is the
effort we voluntarily make to find some order in our
seemingly chaotic lives. Don't gripe about it; WRITE
about it.

"But you don't understand; my life is such a mess." Okay,
then make that mess your message. You probably
can't have a good message without a good mess
anyway. A whole egg in its shell might be
aesthetically appealing, but to make an omelet, you
gotta break and scramble that beautiful egg.

So make your mess your message if that will start you
        writing. Don't gripe; TYPE. Don't whine; WRITE A
        LINE. Writing a little each day will help you develop
        needed discipline. Your writing might not make you
        rich or famous, but it will make you strong and give
        your life discipline, and your life will become
        magically less messy.

2003

A LEAF SMILED

A leaf smiled at me, then fled,
    Dancing gaily down the autumn breeze;
I smiled too, while swiveling my head,
    Watching her swirl away among the trees.

My smile faded, wishing her return,
    As flighty flittings took her out of sight;
Then inward crept a melancholy yearn,
    As I discerned the nearing of the night.

I gazed around to survey other leaves,
    Hoping to find one like that one gone;
Against the growing chill, rolled down my sleeves
    And stood there in the forest all alone.

Others were pretty: orange, gold and red,
    And I admired those others for a while;
However, none was like the one that fled,
    And none could duplicate her matchless smile.

Bill & Thelma Carroll
October, 2003

AUTUMN ORANGE

With the greenness of youth now faded, the true red/gold
beauties of our lives can emerge to full view for greater
appreciation.

We can display the buttery tones of pumpkins and carrots, of
mellowing apples and pears, of so many kinds of gourds
and various winter squashes.

Our lives can be spiced up like the scent of apple cider, like
savory apple butter, like cooling mincemeat pies, like
bronze fat sweet potatoes (cured, baked, fried, pied,
etc.).

The non-native aromas of flown-in fruits, even of exotic
foreign fruits, perfume the days and the dreams of our
autumn.

Unlike the tree leaves that fall and clutter up the lives of
others, we stand steadfast like the trees themselves, and
like those persistent peppers of October and November,
instead of drying and dying, we continue to grow more
beautiful.

November, 2003; revised 2006
Published in *The New Journal and Guide,* 2004

REMEMBER

Remembering reverses dismembering, not taking things apart, but putting them back together. When we re-member, we rejoin or reconnect elements which had become disjointed.

Scenes and events from our past can become severed from us and from each other. Remembering reunites. Of course, we might not wish to remember some scenes and experiences, relive the pain which that remembering brings or prolongs; but if we try to outrun or ignore those memories that hurt us, we may actually increase their pain power.

Remembering those past pains can force us to face them down, can empower us to deal with them so that their power to haunt and taunt and hurt us shrivels like a threatening letter in a cleansing flame. Remember that.

October, 2003
Published in *The New Journal and Guide,* 2004

A PLEA FOR TOLERATION

Three not so little words could form a particularly blessed trinity:
Freedom, Reason, Toleration.

FREEDOM can be a frightening concept, especially for
people who like the comfort and ease of having
decisions made for them. Absolute freedom would
be absolute chaos, so our freedoms must endure
some restrictions. Freedom of religion is one of
our nation's fundamental rights, not just freedom
to do and believe as I do or say, but freedom to
worship (or not) in accord with your own needs
and conscience. Religious freedom, like other
freedoms, comes with accompanying
responsibilities; "The devil made me do it," is
usually not an adequate excuse for irresponsible
deeds done in the name of freedom.

REASON is a God-given gift which we can use to under-
stand and appreciate this magnificent universe
which we occupy and all too often abuse or
ignore. Reason can even help us in comprehending
mysterious happenings that do not seem to play by
the rules of our reason. Call them mysteries,
miracles, or whatever words seem fit. The words
themselves do accord with reason somehow and
help human minds discern some order in what
looks chaotic.

TOLERANCE, especially religious tolerance, is a virtue
which our world can never have in
overabundance. That toleration of which I speak is
not merely a grudging putting up with the other's
religion — not bothering them if they don't bother
us; instead, it is an engaging and examining of
each other's beliefs to the point that we can
benefit from each other's views. I understand that
some religions require adherents to convert others
to their way of thinking and living. Unfortunately,
when carried to extremes, this practice can result
in the most obnoxious of oxymorons: Holy War.
Such conflicts could not occur in a truly tolerant
world. If early New England settlers, who fled
religious persecution in the Old World, had been
tolerant, Rhode Island and Connecticut would still
be parts of Massachusetts. A true spirit of
religious toleration could give the world's
societies the means to learn from all aspects of our
disparate cultures and finally start along the path
to lasting PEACE.

2003

EACH LIFE LIVED

Each life that's lived has meaning, truth and worth;
No life is ever wasted on God's earth.
We might not understand each life's intent,
Nor comprehend why each of us was sent,
But precious Life is meaningfully spent.

Some seem to have been born for only woe,
Not seeming to have lived before they go,
But their lives' purpose did not have to be
The same as one that lived to ninety-three;
Appreciate each treasured memory.

And as we gather in this place today,
And bid farewell to one who's gone away,
Let us be thankful for the lovely weather;
And tho it is to mourn a death we gather,
His life might bring us closer yet – together.

William Carroll — November, 2003
In memory of Adrian Harris (1999-2003)
For the Carolina Carrolls, the Portsmouth Popes,
The Days of Des Moines, and all who revere the
Sacredness of Life.
Published in *The New Journal and Guide,* 2004

THE MAN WHO GROWS

The man who grows to nourish others
    Is a man with a good vision of
The needs and the dreams of his sisters and brothers,
    A man with a heart filled with love.

The man who cultivates the grower's art
    And brings forth good food from the ground
Is a man with a super-size warm loving heart
    Full of blessing that seldom is found.

A man who grows strong in faith and in hope
    And in charity for those left behind
Is one whose strong faith will help us to cope
    With whatever troubles we find.

The man with the knowledge and patience to show
    Young growers to care for the sod
Is a man we can say that we certainly know
    Is a man with a mission from God.

Bill Carroll, Ph. D. — March, 2004
In memory of Deacon Booker T. Smith of
New Light Baptist Church, Virginia Beach, VA –
My Gardening Neighbor and Gardening Mentor, R.I.P.
Published in *The New Journal and Guide,* 2004

REFRACTORY BRIDGE

Like a gigantic multicolored double archway,
It seems to stretch from earth below to heaven above,
And then back down to earth, far away.
Does it form a functional link
Between creatures and Creator?
Can it join today's reality to tomorrow's promise?
Perhaps the really great things about rainbows are —
First, they are beautiful in their own right, and
Second, they can symbolize anything
The human mind can imagine or desire.

2004
Published in *The New Journal and Guide,* 2004

VERNAL EQUINOX

Eliot declared April to be the cruelest month;
Whitman vowed to mourn with ever-returning spring.
All due respect to those honored dead poets,
But, no matter how much we might rue the endings
Of exemplary lives of luminaries such as
Jesus of Nazareth and Lincoln of Illinois,
Do we not have a duty to look at the bigger picture?

Death is a natural and integral part of human physical life
As we know it. It happens to all of us.
Jesus lived and walked as a mortal man;
His cries of anguish during a slow, painful death
Bring pangs of empathy from other mortals,
Even if He did invoke forgiveness for His tormentors.

Though the Son of Man and Honest Abe
Encountered violent tragic deaths in spring or April,
The legacy of love and life that they left
Can teach us all to live lives of love
And to celebrate Spring for the living Love
That doesn't just return with spring,
But lingers and abides in all seasons.

2004

EMPOWERMENT OF TAMBOURINE

Drum forbidden, talking drum;
Inborn rhythms still did come,
Come to cruel hostile lands
In those strong black feet and hands;
People still could stomp and clap,
Despite oppression's savage trap.

Artful hands and clever brains
Worked to bring forth rhythmic strains
Of music to set spirits winging
And the people's souls to singing.
In this ocean of emotion,
The tambourine swung into motion.

Mini-drum, the tambourine,
With ringing, jingling sound so clean,
Its name had once been given to
A comic minstrel figure too,
But in the Celebration Hour,
Miss Tambourine asserts her power.

2004
Published in *The New Journal and Guide,* 2004

NO GREATER LOVE

Greater love hath no man than this,
that a man lay down his life for his friends.
– John 15:13

We take the words of sacrifice to mean
    The greatest love is dying for one's friends;
However, "Lay down life" could also mean
    To LIVE for others, giving 'til the end;
To die might be a loving act all right,
But living lovingly is hardly slight.

All things that live will die, and that's a fact
    We all must face, like it or not;
To die for friends can be a noble act,
    But living for them means that we have got
To keep on dedicating, day and night
Our lives to others, with no end in sight.

December, 2003
Published in *The New Journal and Guide,* 2004

CRITICAL STATEMENT

I strive to make my poetry especially accessible
    Without turning out to appear simple minded as well;
I'd like readers to find all my concepts possessable
    With images ringing through clearly as clarion bells;
Such blending of parts is, however, well nigh impossible.

But I do not throw up my hands in easy surrender,
    Nor give in to stringing together simple trite clichés;
However, rarely will I venture, stray or wander
    To Abstruse-land where readers won't know what I say;
I try to mix words like a master chef subgenre blender.

My free verse frequently flows like just plain bland prose,
    But I do not always view that as a serious fault,
For surely each undergraduate English major knows
    That this technique worked OK for a guy named Walt,
So I'll just keep on keeping on, and keeping on my toes.

This crazy five-line stanza indicates a curious choice
    Which I cannot explain fully – even to myself yet;
It's part of an ongoing search for my particular voice;
    Perhaps I'll ultimately label it the "Carroll Quintet;"
If I can ever settle on meter or scansion, I guess I can rejoice.

Dr. Bill (A Signature Piece)
October, 2003

SONG FOR SUNRISE

On the shore at sunrise
Day fills expectant skies,
And the vision of new life comes to my eyes.
'Way beyond the briny bay
The lively dolphins play
And seem to want to say
This is the proper way to greet the day.

O'er the wakening seaside
Shore birds soar and hang-glide
As they surf and ride above the morning tide.
High up in the waking sky
Majestic eagles fly
While human vessels ply
The dancing waves, and I whisper a sigh.

To my heart at morning
Comes this sacred warning:
"Live this brand-new day on earth for all it's worth."
Now my soul can recognize
Each new day as a prize
Which we must maximize
And our lives organize — if we are wise.

William Carroll – Summer, 2000
Set to music by composer-conductor Adolphus Hailstork, Spring, 2003
Published in *Songs,Scenes...* 2003, In *New Journal & Guide,* 2004

ODE TO THE CODES

Trying to maintain existence while retaining something like
    sanity: Life's so full of numbers and codes running the
    gamut of the alphabet – access codes, area codes,
    digitized passwords, PINs, VINs, zip codes – all the way
    from A to Z, they get us going and coming – and
    standing still.

It's all 'way too much for Old School Minds, especially
    when those old minds mix up and transpose numbers
    anyhow. Einstein had a point: Why memorize some-
    thing if you know how to find it? But carrying around a
    list of social security numbers, phone numbers, credit
    card numbers and other vital statistical information
    could be heaven for identity thieves and hell for Old
    School Codgers.

Generation Next minds seem to thrive on numbers and
    digital data. Will grandkids save grandsires and grand-
    dames in these digital days? Can they dispel the digital
    daze? For the sake of the elders — as well as the future
    — let's hope so.

August, 2002
(A Signature Piece)
Published in *Songs, Scenes and Sentiments,* 2003

A POSSIBLE EPITAPH

I lived my life, I had some fun;
I loved my wife, loved everyone
      With deep heartfelt compassion.
I tried to dance, I sang my song,
And if perchance I did some wrong,
      'Twas not for form or fashion.
The wrongs I did were just the things
That being human sometimes brings;
      I really meant no harm.
I lasted long enough to be
A senior beneficiary —
      And then I bought the farm.

Dr. Bill — May, 2002
(A Signature Piece)
Published in *Songs, Scenes and Sentiments,* 2003

APPENDIX

About the Author

William Carroll is an emeritus professor of English, having spent virtually his entire professional career as a faculty member at Norfolk State University in Virginia. He was given the name "Dr. Bill" in the mid-1980s when his son (William S. Carroll) was a student at the University.

Professor Carroll holds degrees from Norfolk State, Temple University and the University of North Carolina. He has studied and/or taught briefly at other institutions of higher learning.

Despite decades of teaching and writing about other people's poetry, Carroll did not become active in writing poetry himself until after his retirement in 1999. He published his first volume of poems in 2003 and received an award from the Area II ACT-SO Committee of the NAACP for excellence in poetry in 2004.

Among other activities, the author enjoys writing, working with younger writers (What other kind are there?) and helping vegetables and other plants grow in Virginia Beach.

Other Books by William Carroll

Songs, Scenes and Sentiments: Lyrical Works of Dr. Bill, 2003 (Poetry Collection) ISBN 0-8059-9277-4

The Untied Stats on American: And Other Computer Assisted Writing Errors, 2005 (Humorous Reference Book for Writers) ISBN 0-595-35822-5

Made in the USA
Monee, IL
07 July 2026

56551270R00050